For release on delivery
9:45 p.m. EST (6:45 p.m. PST)
November 18, 2016

I0408834

The Global Trade Slowdown and Its Implications for Emerging Asia

Remarks by

Jerome H. Powell

Member

Board of Governors of the Federal Reserve System

at

"CPBS 2016 Pacific Basin Research Conference," sponsored by
the Center for Pacific Basin Studies at the Federal Reserve Bank of San Francisco

San Francisco, California

November 18, 2016

It is a pleasure for me to return to the Center for Pacific Basin Studies here at the San Francisco Fed. The global economy is at a critical juncture today. According to the International Monetary Fund's latest *World Economic Outlook*, global gross domestic product (GDP) is set to grow at only 3.1 percent this year, the lowest rate of growth since the Global Financial Crisis. Investment and productivity remain subdued, despite extremely low and even negative interest rates in many economies.[1] One key aspect of global weakness that is of particular relevance to emerging Asian economies is the sharp slowdown in global trade. This slowdown represents a notable departure from the "normal" times of the past few decades, and is the subject of my remarks today.[2]

More specifically, I will discuss four topics. First, I will review the main features of the global trade slowdown and summarize the evidence on its potential causes. Second, I will examine the special role that structural changes in China appear to be playing in the trade slowdown. Third, I will turn to the implications of this slowdown for economic growth in the region. And, finally, I will offer some views on how Asian economies can respond to the slowdown by rethinking their "export-led growth" paradigm.

---

[1] The *World Economic Outlook's* headline growth numbers aggregate global growth, using PPP-based GDP weights. They also compute growth using GDP weights based on market exchange rates, according to which global growth this year is projected to be even lower, at 2.4 percent.
[2] The views I express here are my own.

Documenting the Global Trade Slowdown and Its Likely Causes

To set the scene, I will review the main features of the recent global trade slowdown. As you can see on the first slide, growth in world trade rebounded after the Great Recession but has slowed substantially since 2011. On a real inflation-adjusted basis, world imports have grown at an average annual rate of less than 3-1/2 percent since 2011, about half the 7 percent pace seen in the eight years prior to the Global Financial Crisis.[3] As illustrated in the next slide, trade is no longer outpacing GDP growth. The share of real world imports in world GDP has been flat at just under 30 percent since 2011 after nearly doubling between 1985 and 2007.[4] This sustained slowing of real trade relative to GDP is quite unusual: Since 1870, trade has generally grown faster than production, outside of wartime and recessionary periods.

Trade has been sluggish almost everywhere. Real trade growth has been lower over the 2011-15 period compared with the 2000-07 period for every G-20 country outside of Japan, where trade growth was constant. The third slide shows that the fall in real import growth in emerging Asia has been particularly pronounced from over 10 percent in the first period to just about 3 percent in the second. But import growth has declined in Latin America and the advanced economies as well.

The next slide shows the differential between real import growth and real GDP growth for the same two periods. For emerging Asia, the differential went from positive to substantially negative, indicating that real import growth slowed to well below real GDP growth. In advanced

---

[3] In principle, data on either world exports or world imports could be used to study global trade, though the two differ in practice. My remarks here focus on import data, which are generally regarded as more reliable at the country level.

[4] The share of *nominal* world imports to *nominal* GDP has actually been declining since 2011, with a particularly sharp drop in 2015, reflecting steep declines in commodity prices.

foreign economies, the differential was just about zero in the more recent period, indicating that real import growth barely kept pace with GDP growth. Trade relative to GDP has held up better, though, in the United States and Latin America.

Is the trade slowdown just another manifestation of slow growth, or is it an independent concern? That depends on the reasons for the slowdown. Weak global growth is surely part of the explanation, as emphasized by several recent empirical studies, including a special chapter on the topic in the latest IMF *World Economic Outlook*.[5] As can be seen in slide 5, global GDP growth has fallen from an average of 3.5 percent before the Global Financial Crisis to about 2.5 percent since its end.

But weak global growth alone does not explain why trade has slowed to about the same pace as GDP after growing faster than GDP for decades. Part of the reason could be that the particular expenditure categories in which international trade flows are concentrated have become especially weak. A stark case in point is the Global Financial Crisis, when plummeting demand for investment and durable goods--two highly traded expenditure categories-- contributed to the sharp 4 percentage point fall in the ratio of world trade to GDP. The special weakness in some components of demand has persisted beyond the crisis and could also explain some of the recent sluggishness in trade relative to GDP. In particular, as you can see from the middle two bars of slide 5, the slowdown in world investment growth--from about 4.5 percent growth before the Global Financial Crisis to only about 3 percent growth since 2011--has been

---

[5] International Monetary Fund (2016a); see also Organization for Economic Co-operation and Development (2016), European Central Bank (2016), and Hoekman (2015).

more pronounced than the slowdown in world GDP growth or in world consumption. But the differences are not huge, suggesting that this explanation can go only so far.

Indeed, research suggests that other factors are also important in accounting for the slowdown in world trade.[6] One such factor is the deceleration in the pace of trade liberalization policies. From the early 1990s through the mid-2000s, trade barriers were coming down rapidly, including the signing of the North American Free Trade Agreement in 1994, the 2001 entry of China into the World Trade Organization, and the 2005 expiration of the multifibre agreement restricting textile imports to the United States and European Union. These changes resulted in the most rapid increases in the trade-to-GDP ratio since 1870. As the pace of trade liberalization has slowed in recent years, perhaps reflecting limits to further gains from trade agreements, it is only natural that the trade-to-GDP ratio should flatten out as well.

Another related factor is the maturation of global value chains. Increased fragmentation of production across international borders--a natural outgrowth of the gains from specialization-- meant more trade for any given value of final production, thus adding to the major expansion in gross trade flows in the 1990s and 2000s. As shown in the next slide, global value chain participation, as measured by the share of foreign value added in world exports, increased substantially during this period. It is quite plausible that the process of increased fragmentation of production across borders is subject to "diminishing returns" and has its natural limits. Consistent with this notion, the trend toward greater product fragmentation has slowed in recent years.

---

[6] See, for example, European Central Bank (2016), Hoekman (2015), Organization for Economic Co-operation and Development (2016), and Lewis and Monarch (2016).

Finally, of course, China looms large in any discussion of the global trade slowdown. Not only is China's trade being affected by all of the factors just discussed, but on-going structural changes within the Chinese economy, including rebalancing toward domestic demand, are exerting an independent effect on world trade flows. So, let's look next at China in more detail.[7]

China

After years of rapid export-led growth, China is now among the world's leaders in both exports and imports. China's exports now account for 14 percent of the world's total, compared with only 4 percent 15 years ago. At the same time, China's industrialization and export model has greatly increased its own demand for imports of raw materials, intermediate inputs, and parts and components. In recent years, however, growth in both Chinese imports and Chinese exports has slowed markedly. These developments have had a significant effect on global trade. One simple way to measure that effect is to consider what would have happened if China's trade had not decelerated. As shown in slide 7, under a counterfactual in which China's trade growth had not slowed relative to its GDP since 2011, global trade would still be growing as a share of GDP.[8]

---

[7] Another explanation that has been put forward for much of the decline in world trade relative to world GDP is an increased weight of EMEs in the contribution to global growth together with the property that EMEs have lower income elasticities of trade than advanced economies do. (See European Central Bank, 2016.) However, more broadly, the literature does not seem to suggest that income elasticities are significantly lower for EMEs (for example, Lui and others, 2013). Also, while trade financing constraints—another potential explanation—played some role during the severe trade slowdown during the Global Financial Crisis, trade financing does not appear to have become more difficult since 2011 and likely has not been a significant factor in the slowdown in recent years.

[8] See Lewis and Monarch (2016) for more details.

China has, of course, been subject to many of the forces I have already discussed. One notable trend, shown by the black line in slide 8, is that Chinese processing exports--that is, re-exports from assembled imported parts and components--as a share of China's total exports have been falling steadily for several years. This trend in part reflects weak global demand, as weaker demand for final goods and services from the advanced economies should have led Chinese processing exports to fall disproportionately. It is also consistent with the deceleration of global supply chain formation.

Although global factors have undoubtedly played a role, however, the evidence suggests that a substantial part of the slowdown in Chinese trade reflects developments that are specific to the Chinese economy and that are likely to exert a lasting imprint on global trade.[9] First, the rapid expansion of China's manufacturing base over the past 15 years--made possible by vast reserves of cheap, rural labor--may simply be reaching its natural limit. Accordingly, we would expect China's manufacturing exports to slow.

Second, China is moving up the sophistication ladder by producing some higher value-added parts and components itself, instead of importing them. One manifestation of this phenomenon is the higher domestic value-added in Chinese exports in recent years, shown by the gray bars in this slide, relative to the period before the Global Financial Crisis. Another manifestation can be seen in slide 9, which shows the decline in the share of parts and

---

[9] A recent note from the Banque du France--Gaullier, Steingress, and Zignago (2016)--argues that the long run elasticity of world trade to income is unity, and that structural changes in China go a long way in explaining both the sharp rise in the elasticity in the years before the Global Financial Crisis and the subsequent decline in the post-crisis years as China rebalances toward domestic demand.

components in China's total manufactured imports from about 65 percent in 2005 to under 50 percent in 2014.[10] These two pieces of evidence suggest that the shift away from parts and components in Chinese imports is not just due to lower orders tied to weak import demand in the advanced economies, but also due to the rising productivity and sophistication of the Chinese labor force, which is enabling China to move to higher value-added exports.

As China moves up the sophistication ladder, you would also expect other countries to take a greater role in the lower steps of the ladder. We do have evidence that some other countries with cheaper labor, such as Vietnam and Bangladesh, are playing more of a role as exporters in the low-value added parts of the Asian supply chain. Anecdotal evidence suggests, though, that some of this shift is also taking place within China, as low-value-added production shifts to low-wage areas in China's interior.[11]

The third important structural change affecting Chinese trade is the progress China is making in moving away from its export-led model of economic growth and rebalancing its economy toward domestic demand. As shown in slide 10, investment, which in much of the pre-crisis period was supporting high exports, has been falling as a share of the economy in recent years while the consumption share has been rising. Note, though, that the consumption share remains well below its value in the early 2000s. In addition, as can be seen in slide 11, as part of its rebalancing, Chinese production has been shifting away from manufacturing to

---

[10] This share has been computed by updating the methodology followed in Haltmaier and others (2007), which, in turn, extended the methodology of Athukorala and Yamashita (2006).
[11] See, for example, The Economist (2015).

services. Thanks in part to these developments, China's current account surplus (not shown here) has fallen sharply as a share of its GDP over the past several years.[12]

These are welcome developments as China's huge trade surplus created an unsustainable situation, contributing both to internal imbalances within the Chinese economy and to global imbalances. But the rebalancing toward domestic demand will likely put a damper on China's trade for some time as resources shift away from trade-intensive manufacturing. In principle, this drag on China's trade could be partly or even completely offset by stronger imports by Chinese consumers. Evidence of a shift toward imports of consumer goods, however, is limited thus far, and further substantial progress depends on the Chinese authorities' ability to remove distortions that currently depress consumption and boost saving. It may well be, however, that the rising power of the Chinese consumer will in time propel another long round of rapid increases in world trade.

Implications for Growth in the Region

Having examined developments in world and Chinese trade, let me turn to the implications of these trends for economic growth in the emerging Asia region.

There is little doubt that for many years China and other emerging Asian economies have benefited from rapid expansion of trade.[13] Greater trade can provide a host of economic benefits, including enabling the pursuit of comparative advantage, fostering more competition (which leads to more efficiency), generating technological and knowledge spillovers, and facilitating

---

[12] Over the past couple of years, though, China's current account surplus has turned up again, especially as a share of world GDP.

[13] See, for example, Glick and Moreno (1997), Page (1994), and World Bank (1993).

import of key capital goods. These factors enhance productivity and growth and result in the availability of a greater variety of goods to consumers at lower prices. It is safe to say that over the years, the Asian economies have benefited from their high degree of export orientation through all of these transmission mechanisms.[14] A number of academic studies have found a causal link between openness and growth.[15] A simple scatter plot of economic growth across countries over the period from 2000 to 2007 against their export orientation, presented in slide 12, is telling: More trade-intensive economies have grown significantly faster over this period, and the fast-growing emerging Asian economies shown by the red dots have generally been among the most export-oriented.

How did greater focus on trade develop in Asia? At first, increased export orientation in Asia was achieved by taking advantage of low-cost, low-skilled labor to produce low value-added products for foreign markets. Over time, countries such as Japan and South Korea moved up to higher value-added exports, in part through technological and knowledge spillovers. Later, with the rise of China, many emerging Asian economies became integrated into global supply chains, with China acting as the endpoint of a giant Asian assembly line.

Given that trade benefited the Asian economies on the way up, it seems natural that the slowdown in global trade, whatever its causes, could lead to some loss of dynamism and growth in the region. For China, the shift away from trade dependence is partly a reflection of policy choice, with rebalancing seen as a way to sustain growth in the face of some exhaustion of the

---

[14] Some--Page (1994), for example--have argued that industrial policies favoring certain export industries have also played an important role in Asia's success, but it seems to be generally agreed that industrial support was only maintained conditional on successful performance on world markets.
[15] See, for example, Frankel and Romer (1999) and Baldwin (2004).

heavy export/investment model. But many other Asian economies' fortunes are tied to those of China, so developments in China will have important implications for growth in these economies.

One natural question is how the rise in domestic content of Chinese exports is affecting countries that rely heavily on supplying parts and components to China. To document this reliance, your next slide shows that the share of parts and components in other Asian economies' exports to China (the middle green bars) is much greater than their share in exports to the rest of the world (the right blue bars). Over time, this share has fallen from about 70 percent in 2005 to 60 percent in 2014, without the share of parts and components in exports to the rest of the world increasing. This evidence, combined with the evidence I presented earlier on trends in Chinese processing exports, suggests that other economies in Asia are being adversely affected both by less final global demand for Chinese exports and by less use of imported parts and components by China in the production of any given amount of final goods exports.

And the effects of these shifts in supply chains are being offset only very slowly and to only a very limited extent by China importing more goods for domestic consumption.[16] Accordingly, it is doubtful that, at least so far, China is fully replacing advanced-economy demand as an engine of growth for the rest of emerging Asia. One way to look more concretely at this issue is to estimate an equation for the growth for emerging Asia ex. China that separately controls for the effects of Chinese growth and advanced-economy growth. This approach lets us

---

[16] The arguments laid out here are consistent with the findings in the chapter on spillovers from China's transition presented in the latest IMF *World Economic Outlook* (2016b). This chapter concludes that for many countries the effect of China's transition and rebalancing toward a more sustainable growth model will entail short-run negative spillovers, but there will be potential gains to the global economy over the longer term.

see the direct contribution of Chinese growth to that of its neighbors at the margin, apart from the indirect effect due to China's exports to advanced economies.

The results of such an exercise, based on 10-year rolling regressions, are presented in slide 14. Note that in the first half of the 2000s, the effect of advanced-economy growth on emerging Asia ex. China (shown on the left) steadily rises from near zero to a one-to-one effect by 2005, whereas the coefficient on Chinese growth (on the right) hovers around 0.25 and is statistically insignificant. These results suggest that the effect of the rise in China on the rest of emerging Asia in the 2000s mainly reflected China's role as a "conduit" for trade with the advanced economies. However, after the Global Financial Crisis, we see the coefficient on advanced-economy growth move down some, whereas the coefficient on China's growth rises to 0.5 and becomes statistically significant. But the direct effect of advanced-economy growth is still larger than the direct effect of Chinese growth, consistent with the idea that it is still early days for the rebalancing of China's economy and that China will only slowly supplant the role of advanced economies as drivers of emerging Asian growth.

Rethinking the "Export-Led Growth" Paradigm

That brings me to the final topic of my remarks today, which is how emerging Asia can respond to the global trade slowdown and the structural changes taking place in China. Some of the structural changes I have discussed suggest that the recent deceleration of trade relative to GDP will likely persist and that we may expect global trade to grow perhaps about as fast as, but not substantially faster than, global GDP growth for the foreseeable future. Under these circumstances, emerging Asian countries may not be able to look to their export sectors as the key source of dynamism for their economies.

So what's an Asian economy to do? I would argue that, instead of trying to restore growth through enhancing external surpluses, under the circumstances it makes more sense for emerging Asia to focus on domestic demand as an engine of its growth, and to allow their trade and current account surpluses to shrink. When looking at these economies in aggregate, as shown in your next slide, current account surpluses narrowed greatly after the Global Financial Crisis but rebounded substantially thereafter.[17] However, as you can see in slide 16, we have seen some narrowing of current account balances as a share of GDP in several emerging Asian economies, although in some others, such as South Korea, Taiwan, and Thailand, the surpluses have increased. Encouraging domestic demand and allowing for downward adjustment of these surpluses in emerging Asia, with more balances turning into deficits, would provide a much-needed injection of demand into the global economy and also support economic growth in the region by providing another source of growth in place of the lessened impetus from external demand.

A shift toward external deficits in Asia would be advantageous, considering the low level of external financing costs at present. Many observers are raising the possibility of a "new normal" for the global economy, in which moderate global demand, low productivity growth, and slow trade may persist for some time, keeping interest rates in the advanced economies "low for long." To be sure, bond yields have moved up recently, but they remain quite low by historical standards. Accordingly, the cost of external finance to Asian economies has fallen, which should support strong private capital flows to emerging markets. Normally, we would

---

[17] See Setster (2016) for a detailed discussion of the return of the East Asian savings glut.

worry about volatility of these flows and how they might exacerbate risks of financial instability, particularly as U.S. monetary policy normalizes. But we should also bear in mind that many emerging market economies (EMEs), particularly in Asia, have improved their macroeconomic fundamentals over the past two decades; that they have built an adequate war chest of reserves, with no pending need to further reserve accumulation for precautionary purposes; and that their currencies are much more flexible, which acts as an adjustment mechanism to shocks and also lessens the possibility of fluctuations in reserves due to currency intervention. These factors have made the emerging Asian economies much less vulnerable.

Given all this, dare we imagine a world in which private capital inflows to EMEs could prove self-sustaining, are not offset by reverse flows of official capital, and would finance long-term profitable investment that would help support growth in these economies while also supporting global growth? In essence, these capital inflows would finance the shift from export-led growth to domestic-led growth required by the slowdown in global trade. And, with little or no official outflows, EMEs would have total capital net inflows as well, consistent with running current account deficits instead of current account surpluses. As pointed out recently by former Fed Chairman Ben Bernanke, the availability of profitable capital investments in one part of the world can help defeat secular stagnation in another part.[18]

Of course, these developments may take time. The point is that at this current juncture of the global economy, it is all the more important for emerging Asian economies—and, indeed, emerging market economies more broadly—to enhance domestic demand while pursuing

---

[18] See Bernanke (2015).

prudent policies. It would be good to do this for the sake of the global economy, but emerging Asian economies should do this for their own sakes as well.

(Thank you. I would be happy to take a few questions.)

References

Athukorala, Prema-Chandra, and Nobuaki Yamashita (2006). "Production Fragmentation and Trade Integration: East Asia in a Global Context," *North American Journal of Economics and Finance,* vol. 17 (3), pp. 233-56.

Baldwin, Robert E. (2004). "Openness and Growth: What's the Empirical Relationship?" in Robert E. Baldwin and L. Alan Winers, eds., *Challenges to Globalization: Analyzing the Economics.* Chicago: University of Chicago Press, February, pp. 499-525, www.nber.org/chapters/c9548.pdf.

Bernanke, Ben (2015). "Why Are Interest Rates So Low, Part 2: Secular Stagnation," Brookings Institute, March 31, www.brookings.edu/blog/ben-bernanke/2015/03/31/why-are-interest-rates-so-low-part-2-secular-stagnation/.

The Economist (2015). "A Tightening Grip: Rising Chinese Wages Will Only Strengthen Asia's Hold on Manufacturing," *The Economist,* March 14, www.economist.com/news/briefing/21646180-rising-chinese-wages-will-only-strengthen-asias-hold-manufacturing-tightening-grip.

European Central Bank (2016). "Understanding the Weakness in Global Trade. What is the New Normal?" European Central Bank Occasional Paper Series No. 178, September, www.ecb.europa.eu/pub/pdf/scpops/ecbop178.en.pdf.

Frankel, Jeffrey, and David Romer (1999). "Does Trade Cause Growth?" *American Economic Review,* vol. 89 (June), pp. 379-99.

Gaulier, Guillaume, Walter Steingress, and Soledad Zignago (2016). "The Role of China in the Trade Slowdown," *Rue de la Banque,* Banque de France, No. 30 (September).

Glick, Reuven, and Ramon Moreno (1997). "The East Asian Miracle: Growth because of Government Intervention and Protectionism or in Spite of It?" *Business Economics,* vol. 32 (April), pp. 20-5.

Haltmaier, Jane T., Shaghil Ahmed, Brahima Coulibaly, Ross Knippenberg, Sylvain Leduc, Mario Marazzi, and Beth Anne Wilson. (2007). "The Role of China in Asia: Engine, Conduit, or Steamroller?" International Finance Discussion Papers 904. Board of Governors of the Federal Reserve System, September, www.federalreserve.gov/pubs/ifdp/2007/904/ifdp904.pdf.

Hoekman, Bernard, ed. (2015). *The Global Trade Slowdown: A New Normal?* VoxEU.org eBook. London: Centre for Economic Policy Research, June, http://voxeu.org/sites/default/files/file/Global%20Trade%20Slowdown_nocover.pdf.

International Monetary Fund (2016a). *World Economic Outlook,* chapter 2: *Global Trade: What's behind the Slowdown?* Washington, D.C.: IMF, October, www.imf.org/external/pubs/ft/weo/2016/02/#ch2.

------ (2016b). *World Economic Outlook*, chapter 4: *Spillovers from China's Transition and from Migration.* Washington, D.C.: IMF, October, www.imf.org/external/pubs/ft/weo/2016/02/#ch4.

Lewis, Logan, and Ryan Monarch (2016). "Causes of the Global Trade Slowdown," IFDP Notes (Washington: Board of Governors of the Federal Reserve System, November), www.federalreserve.gov/econresdata/notes/ifdp-notes/2016/causes-of-the-global-trade-slowdown-20161110.html.

Lui, Silvia, Rebecca Riley, Dawn Holland, Ali Orazgani, and Pawel Paluchowski (2013). "Long Run Income Elasticities of Import Demand," BIS Research Paper No. 144. London: National Institute of Economic and Social Research, www.gov.uk/government/uploads/system/uploads/attachment_data/file/252490/bis-13-1262-long-run-income-elasticities-REVISED-1.pdf.

Organisation for Economic Co-operation and Development (2016). "Cardiac Arrest or Dizzy Spell: Why Is World Trade So Weak and What Can Policy Do about It?" OECD Economic Policy Papers, No. 18. Washington, D.C.: OECD, September, www.oecd.org/eco/outlook/Cardiac-arrest-or-dizzy-spell-why-is-world-trade-so-weak-OECD-Paris-21-September-2016.pdf.

Page, John (1994). "The East Asian Miracle: Four Lessons for Development Policy," in Stanley Fischer and Julio Rotemberg, eds., *NBER Macroeconomic Annual*, vol. 9 (January), pp. 219-82.

Setser, Brad (2016). "The Return of the East Asian Savings Glut," CFR Discussion Paper. Council on Foreign Relations, October, www.cfr.org/asia-and-pacific/return-east-asian-savings-glut/p38417.

World Bank (1993). *The East Asian Miracle: Economic Growth and Public Policy.* New York: Oxford University Press.

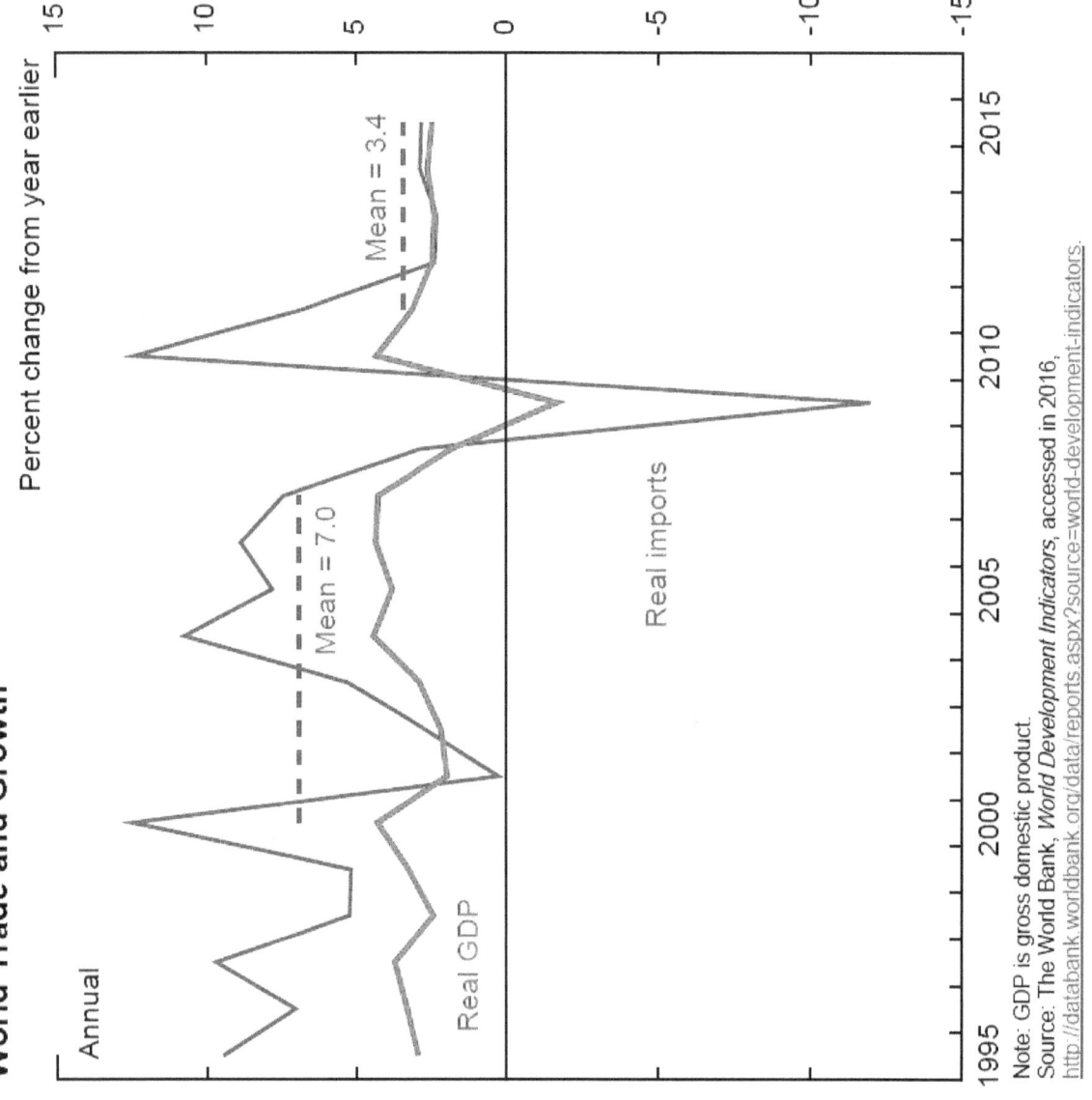

Slide 1

Slide 2

World Trade as a Share of GDP

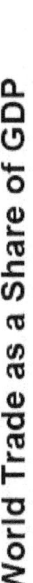

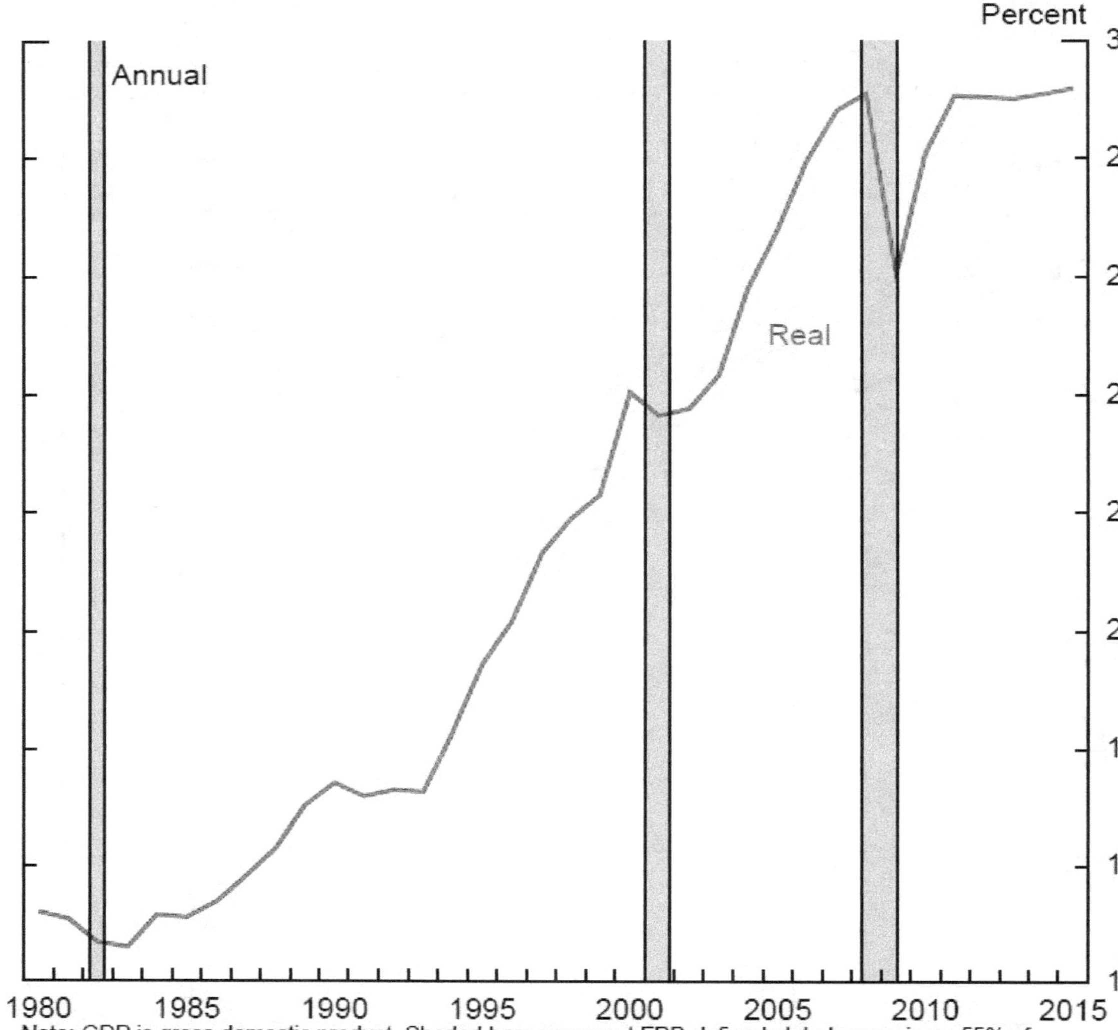

Percent

Annual

Real

Note: GDP is gross domestic product. Shaded bars represent FRB-defined global recessions: 55% of world GDP in recession.
Source: The World Bank, *World Development Indicators*, accessed in 2016, http://databank.worldbank.org/data/reports.aspx?source=world-development-indicators.

Slide 3

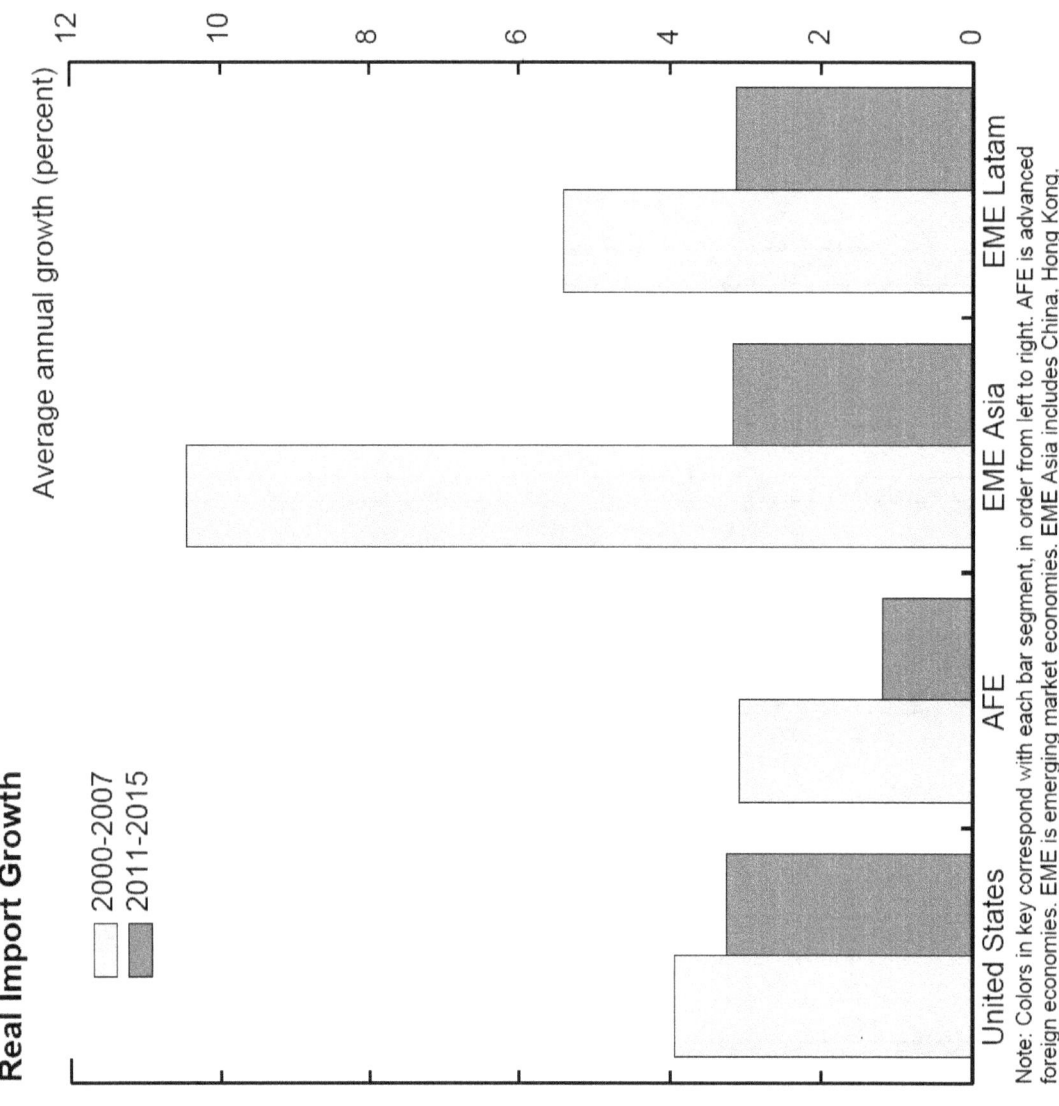

Real Import Growth

Average annual growth (percent)

Legend: 2000-2007, 2011-2015

United States   AFE   EME Asia   EME Latam

Note: Colors in key correspond with each bar segment, in order from left to right. AFE is advanced foreign economies. EME is emerging market economies. EME Asia includes China, Hong Kong, Indonesia, Malaysia, Philippines, Singapore, South Korea, Taiwan, and Thailand. EME Latam includes Argentina, Brazil, Chile, Colombia, Mexico, and Venezuela.

Source: FRB staff calculations; Netherlands Bureau of Policy Analysis, World Trade Monitor, accessed in 2016, http://www.cpb.nl/en/data.

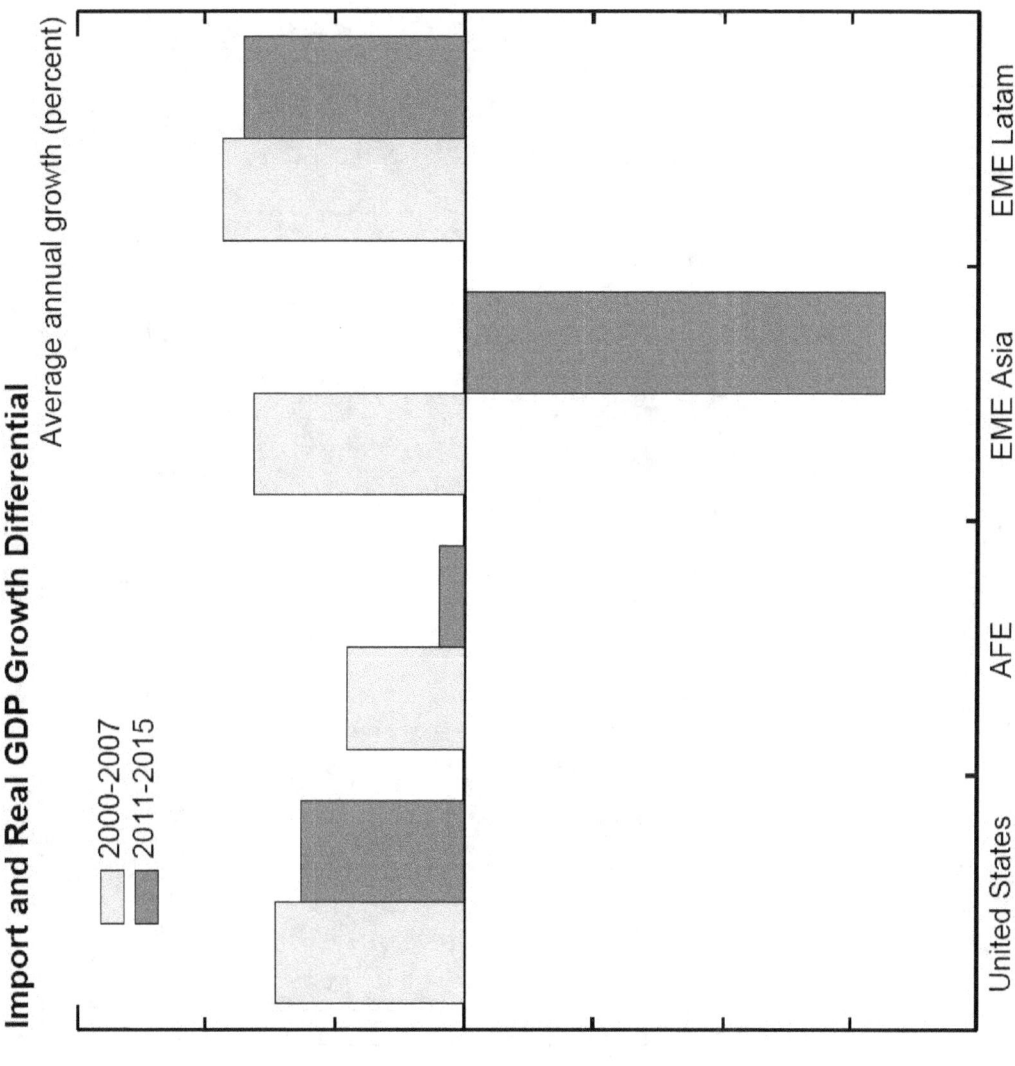

Import and Real GDP Growth Differential

Average annual growth (percent)

2000-2007
2011-2015

United States   AFE   EME Asia   EME Latam

Note: Colors in key correspond with each bar segment, in order from left to right. GDP is gross domestic product. AFE is advanced foreign economies. EME is emerging market economies. EME Asia includes China, Hong Kong, Indonesia, Malaysia, Philippines, Singapore, South Korea, Taiwan, and Thailand. EME Latam includes Argentina, Brazil, Chile, Colombia, Mexico, and Venezuela. Source: FRB staff calculations; Netherlands Bureau of Policy Analysis, World Trade Monitor, accessed in 2016, http://www.cpb.nl/en/data.

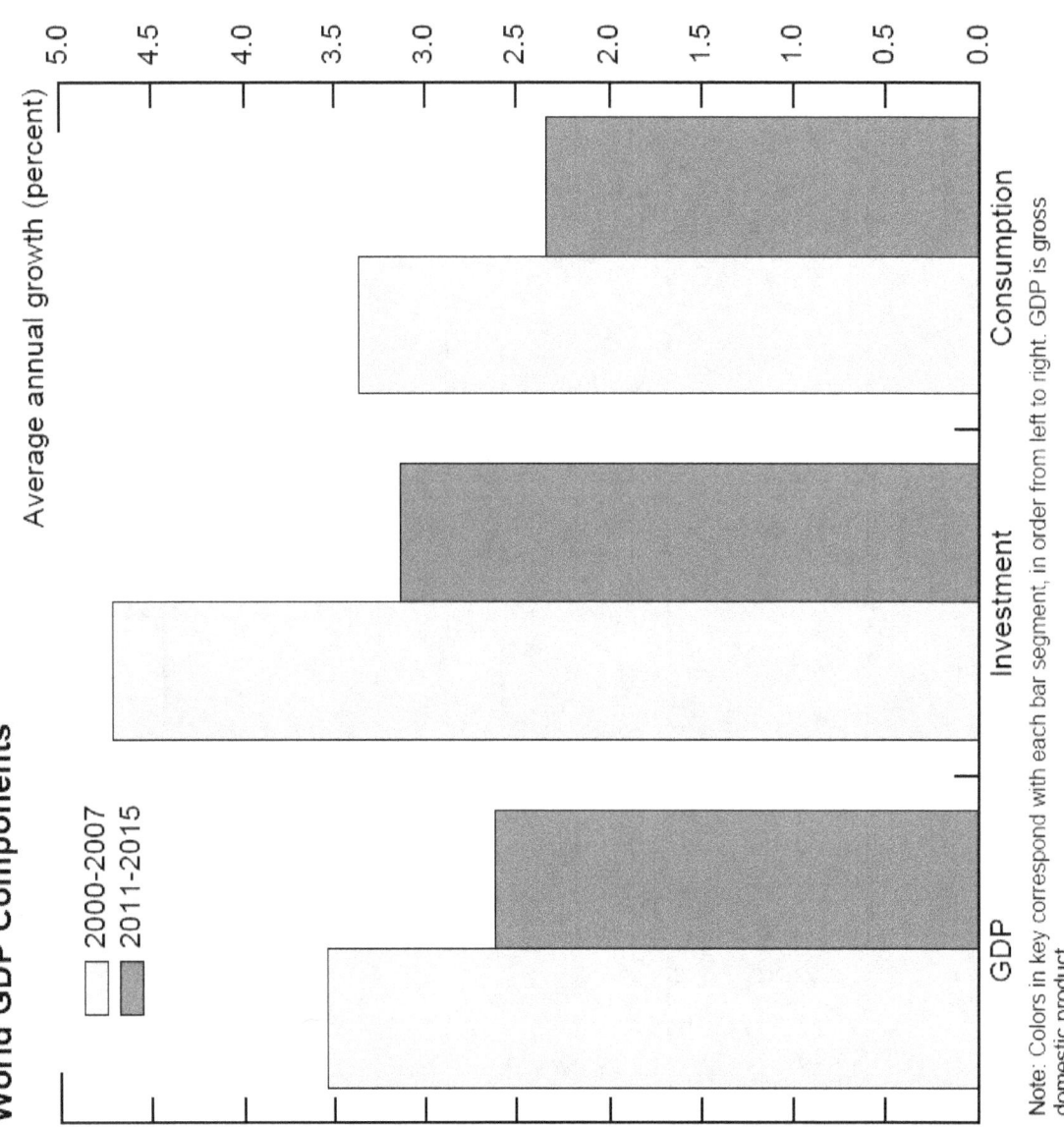

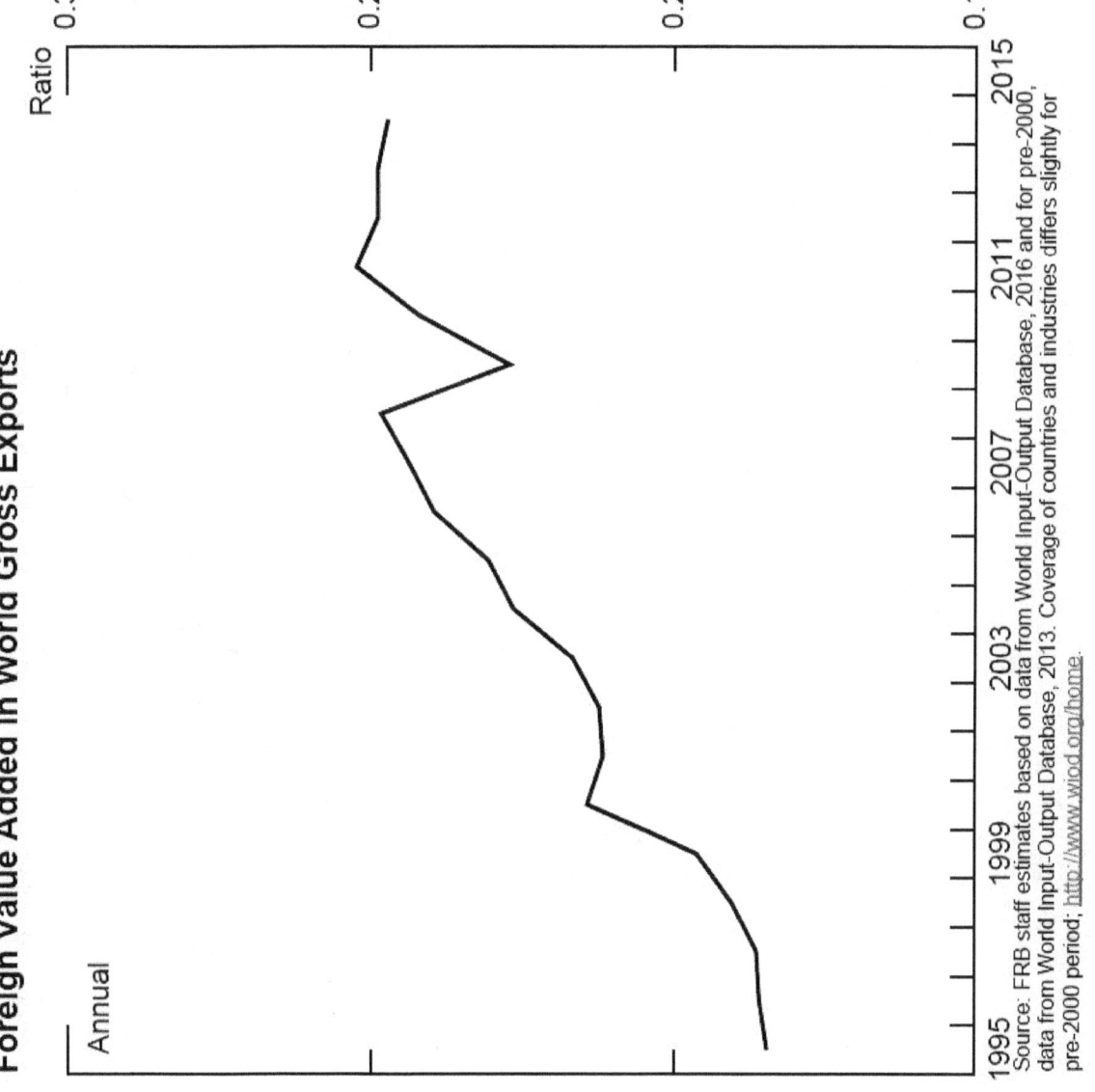

Foreign Value Added in World Gross Exports

Annual

Ratio

Source: FRB staff estimates based on data from World Input-Output Database, 2016 and for pre-2000, data from World Input-Output Database, 2013. Coverage of countries and industries differs slightly for pre-2000 period; http://www.wiod.org/home.

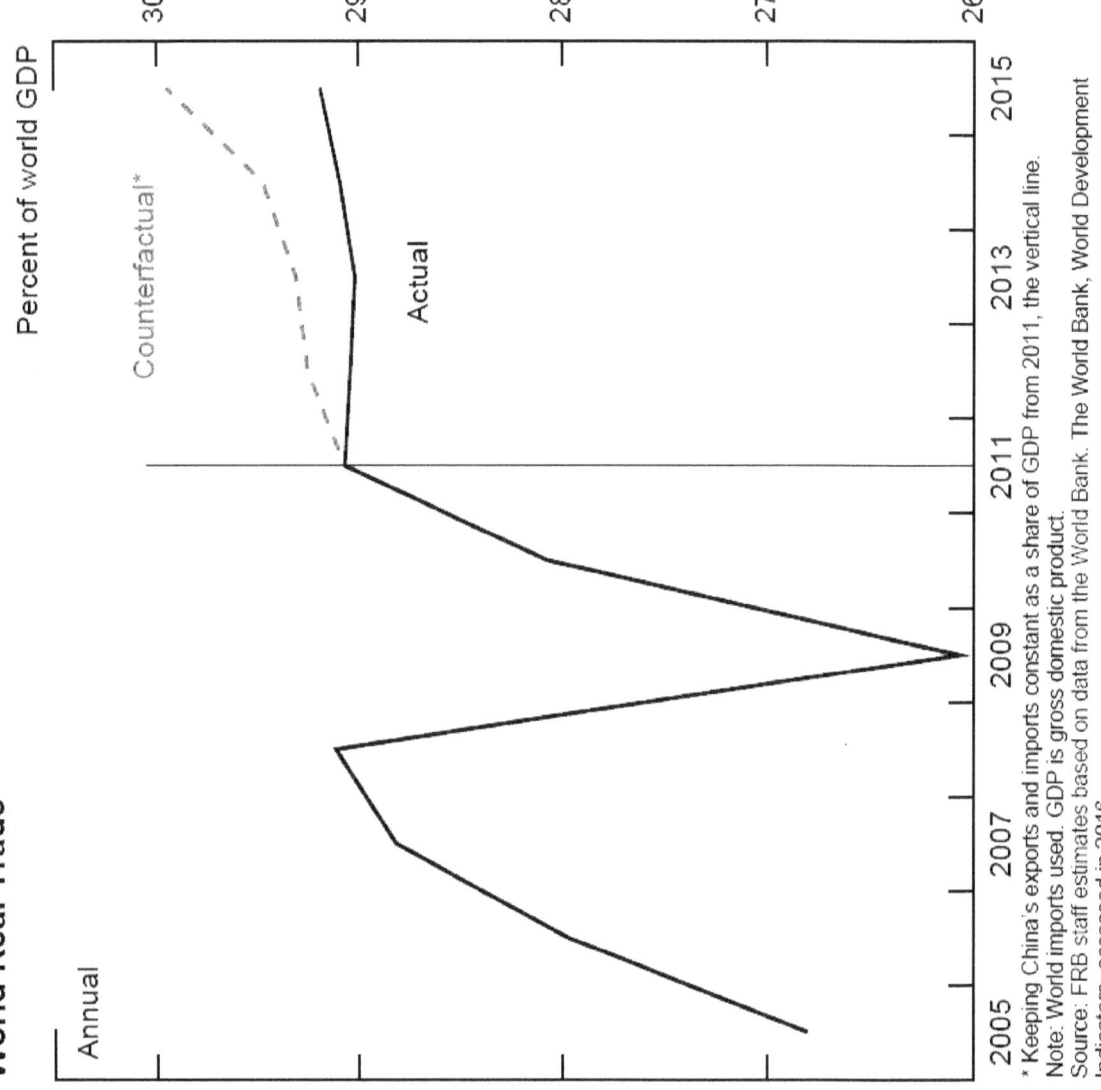

Slide 7

World Real Trade

Annual

Percent of world GDP

* Keeping China's exports and imports constant as a share of GDP from 2011, the vertical line.
Note: World imports used. GDP is gross domestic product.
Source: FRB staff estimates based on data from the World Bank. The World Bank, World Development Indicators, accessed in 2016, http://databank.worldbank.org/data/reports.aspx?source=world-development-indicators.

Slide 8

China's Processing Trade

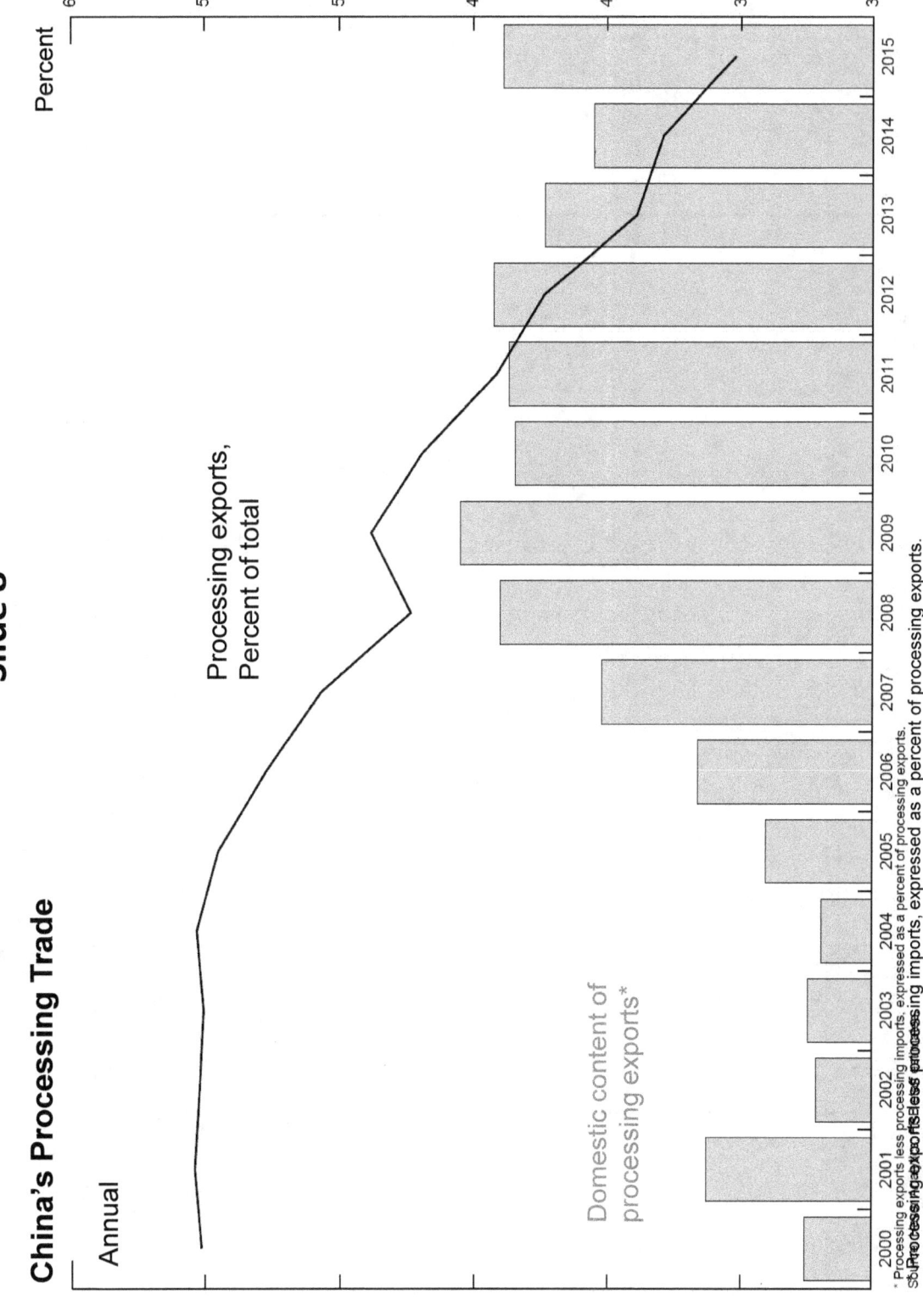

Annual

Percent

Processing exports,
Percent of total

Domestic content of
processing exports*

* Processing exports less processing imports, expressed as a percent of processing exports.
Source: Haver Analytics; FRB staff estimates.

Slide 9

China: Imports of Parts and Components
Percent of total manufactured imports

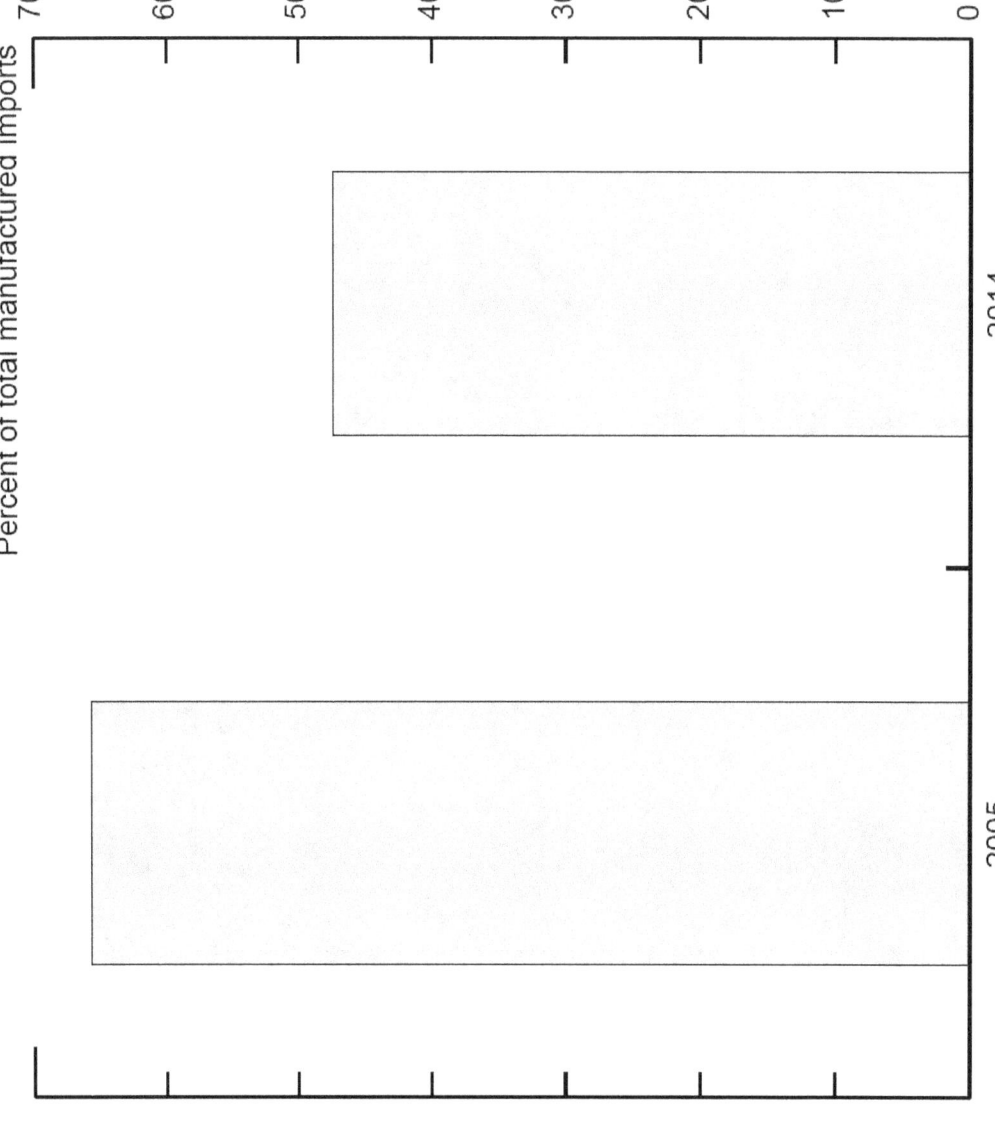

2005   2014

70

60

50

40

30

20

10

0

Note: China includes Hong Kong.
Source: FRB staff estimates based on Commodity Trade Statistics database (Comtrade), updated
using the methodology of Haltmaier et. al (2007). United Nations, Comtrade, Department of Economic
and Social Affairs / Statistics Division, http://comtrade.un.org/db/.

Slide 10

China's Rebalancing: Demand

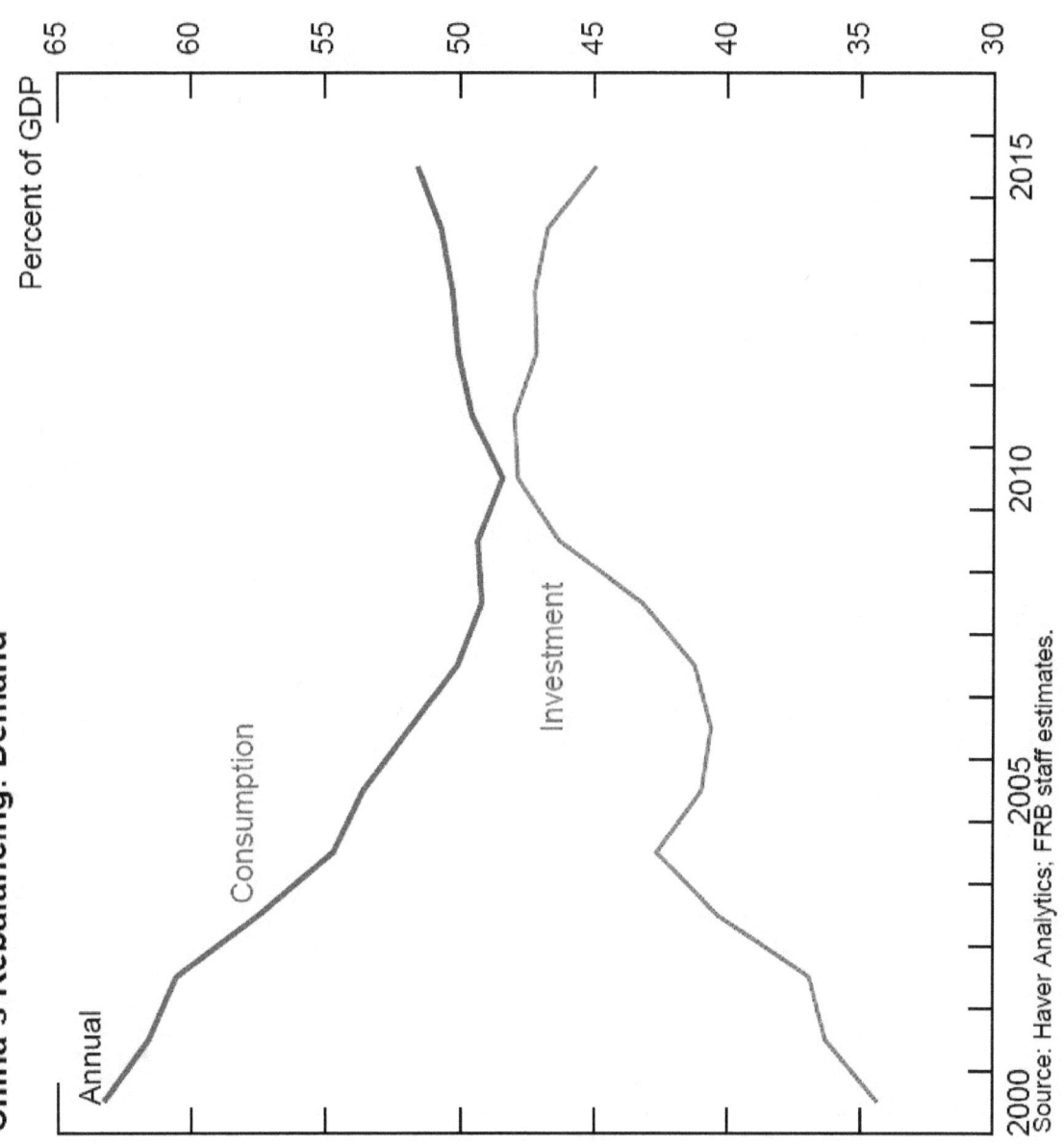

Source: Haver Analytics; FRB staff estimates.

Slide 11

China's Rebalancing: Supply

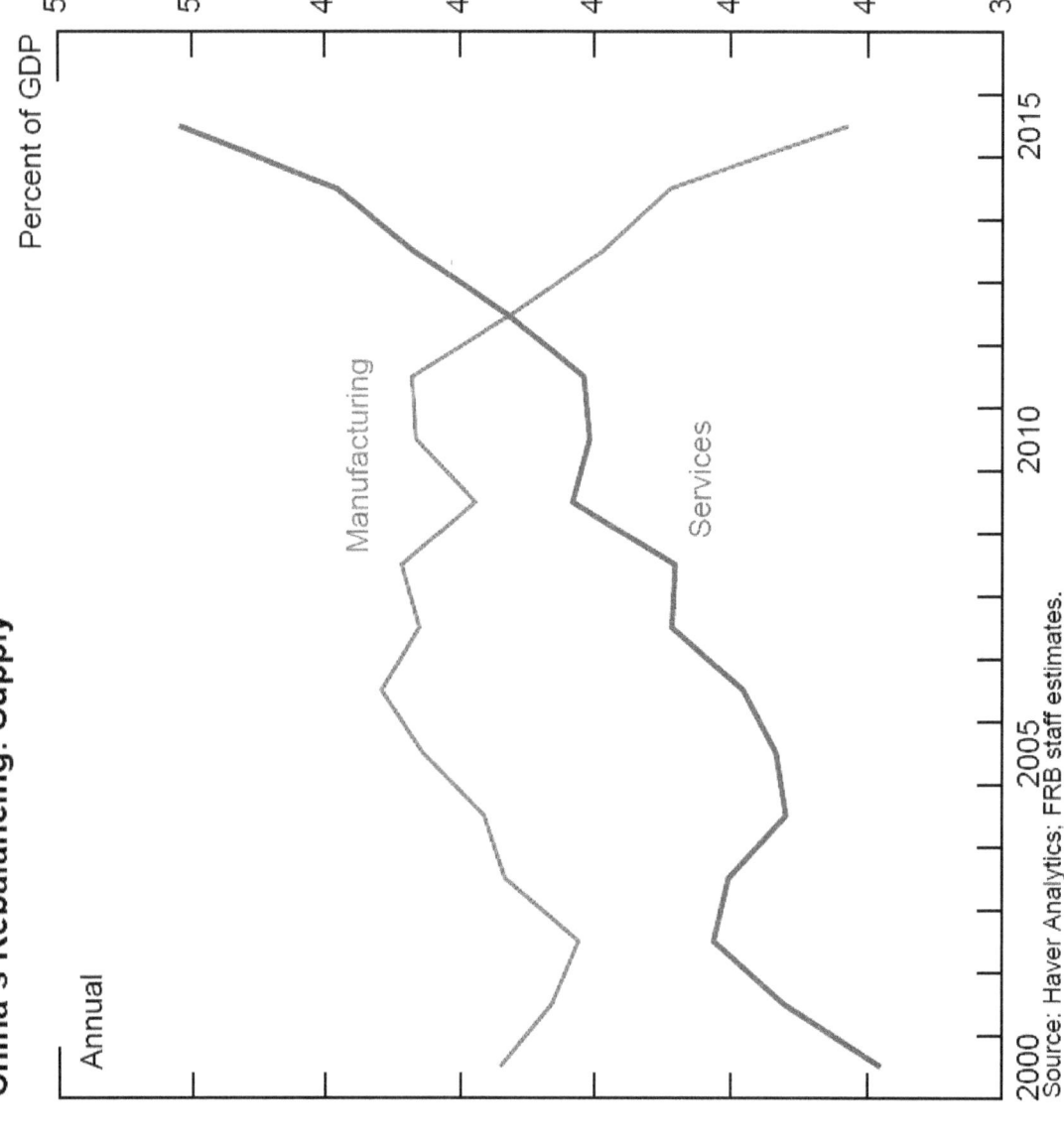

Source: Haver Analytics; FRB staff estimates.

Slide 12

Growth and Export Orientation

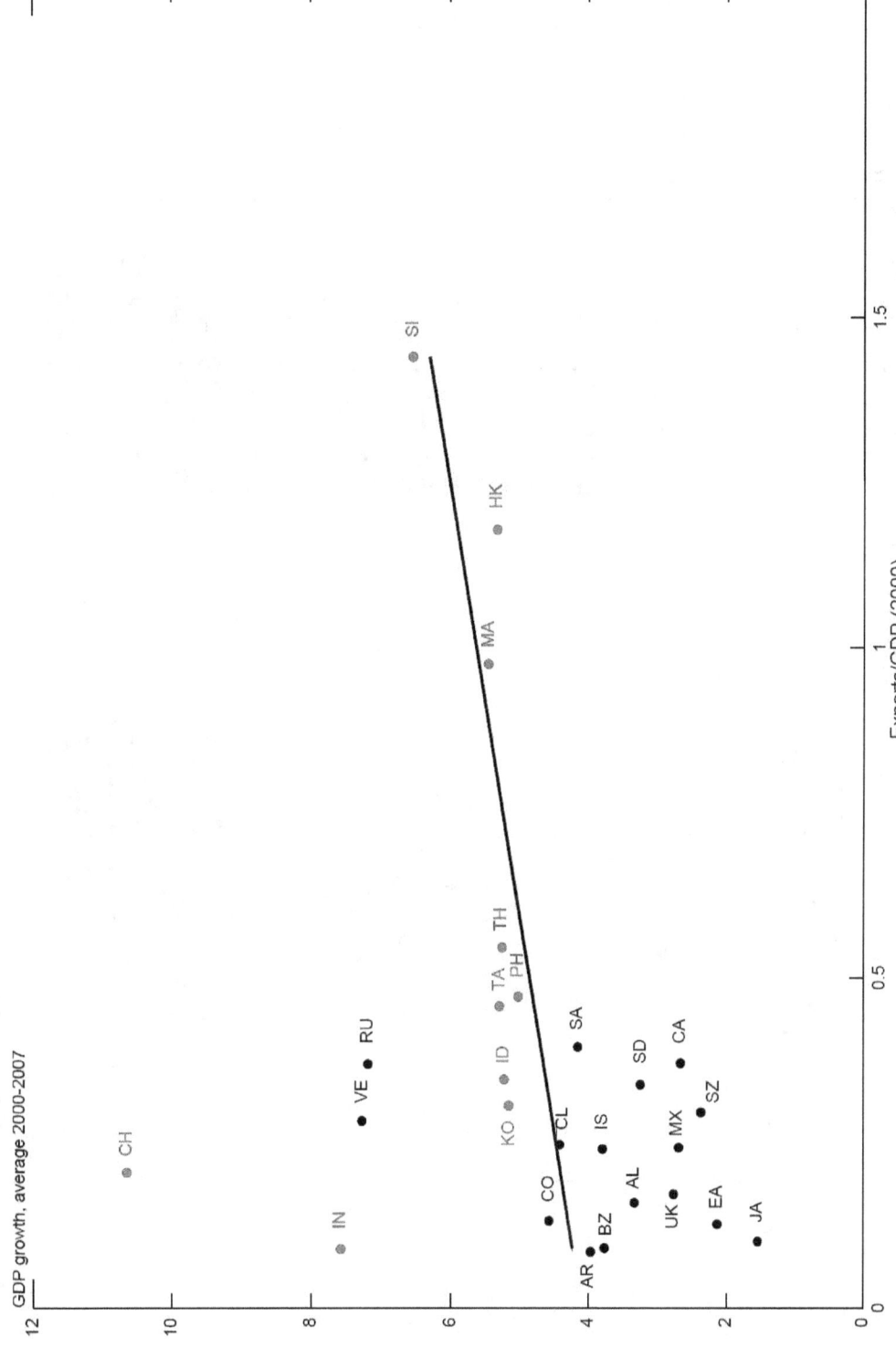

Note: GDP is gross domestic product. Line is the regression fit line including all countries. AL=Australia. AR=Argentina. BZ=Brazil. CA=Canada. CH=China. CL=Chile. CO=Colombia. EA=Euro area.
HK=Hong Kong. ID=Indonesia. IN=India. IS=Israel. JA=Japan. KO=South Korea. MA=Malaysia. MX=Mexico. PH=Philippines. RU=Russia. SA=Saudi Arabia. SI=Singapore. SZ=South Africa.
TA=Taiwan. TH=Thailand. VE=Venezuela. UK=United Kingdom.
Source: FRB staff estimates based on data from Haver Analytics and World Economic Outlook Database (April 2016).

Slide 13

Asia ex. China: Parts and Components Exports

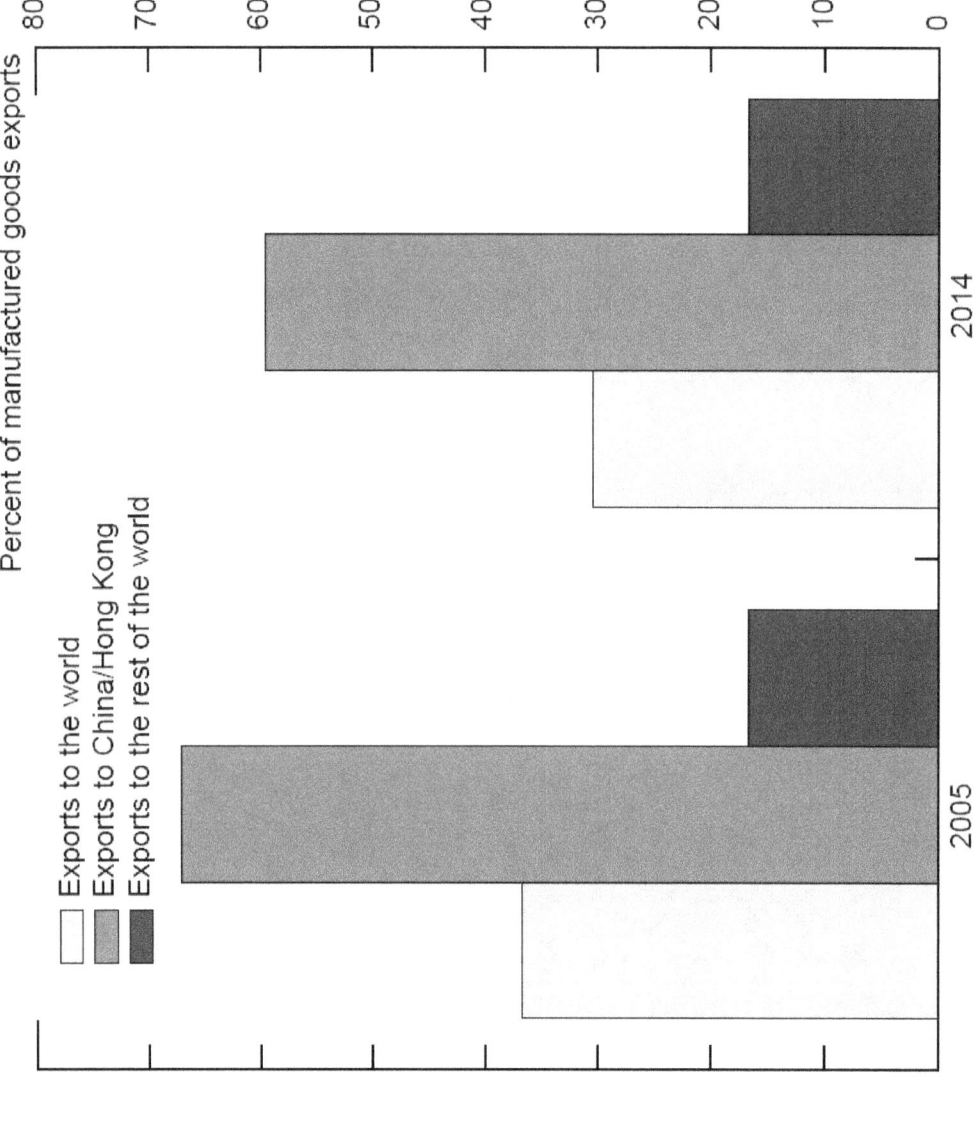

Percent of manufactured goods exports

Exports to the world
Exports to China/Hong Kong
Exports to the rest of the world

2005   2014

Slide 14

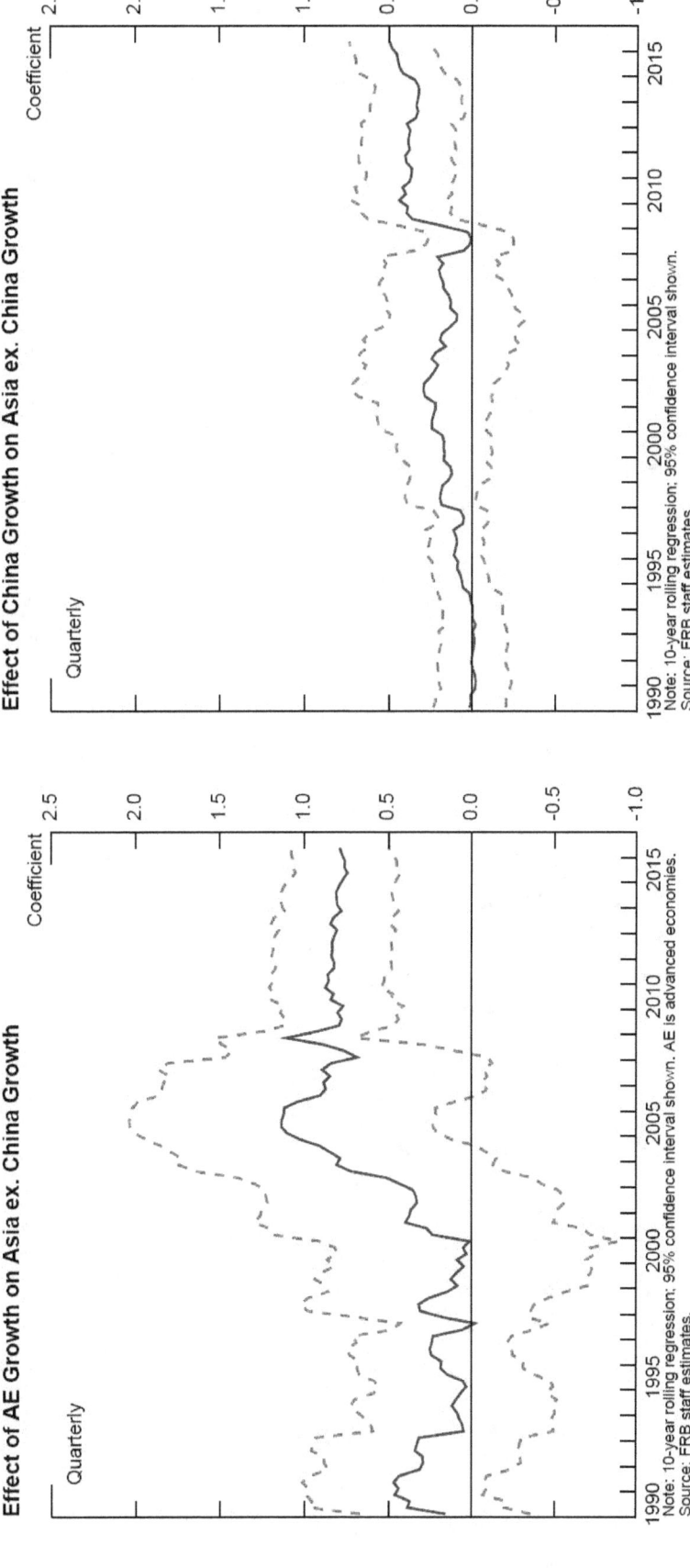

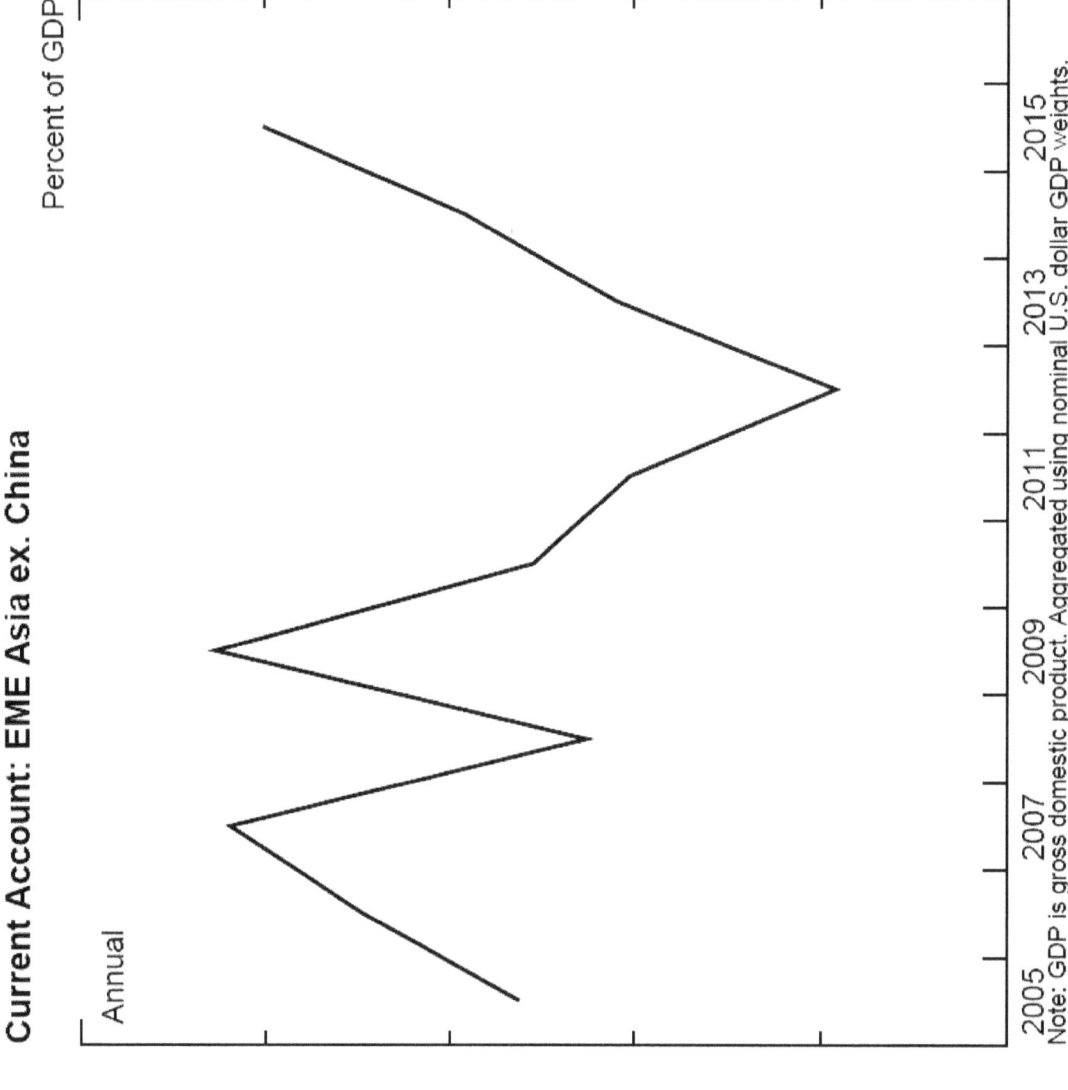

Slide 15

Current Account: EME Asia ex. China

Annual

Percent of GDP

2005   2007   2009   2011   2013   2015

Note: GDP is gross domestic product. Aggregated using nominal U.S. dollar GDP weights.
Includes Hong Kong, India, Indonesia, South Korea, Malaysia, Philippines, Singapore,
Taiwan, and Thailand.
Source: Haver Analytics; FRB staff estimates.

Slide 16

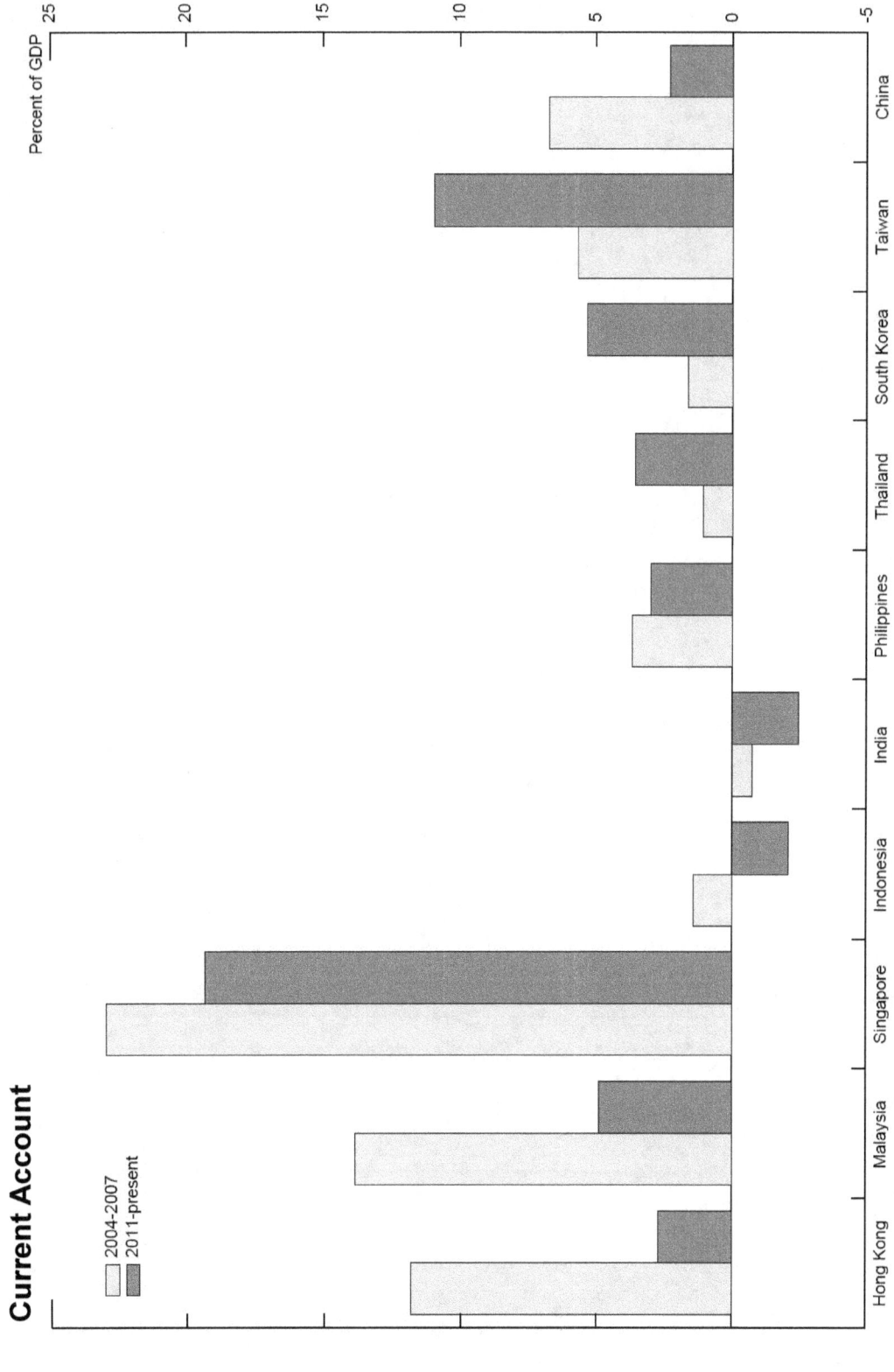

Current Account

Note: Colors in key correspond with each bar segment, in order from left to right.
Source: Haver Analy ics; The World Bank, World Development Indicators, accessed in 2016, http://databank.worldbank.org/data/repors.aspx?source=world-development-indicators.